BXJC

Military Amphibious Vehicles

by Grace Hansen

Abdo

MILITARY AIRCRAFT & VEHICLES

Kids

abdopublishing.com

Published by Abdo Kids, a division of ABDO, PO Box 398166, Minneapolis, Minnesota 55439.

Copyright © 2017 by Abdo Consulting Group, Inc. International copyrights reserved in all countries. No part of this book may be reproduced in any form without written permission from the publisher.

Printed in the United States of America, North Mankato, Minnesota.

102016

012017

 THIS BOOK CONTAINS RECYCLED MATERIALS

Photo Credits: Depositphotos Enterprise, Images of Freedom, iStock, marines.mil, navy.mil, ©FotograFFF p.cover, ©Popsuievych p.19, ©Johnny Dao p.22 / Shutterstock.com

Production Contributors: Teddy Borth, Jennie Forsberg, Grace Hansen

Design Contributors: Laura Mitchell, Dorothy Toth

Publisher's Cataloging in Publication Data

Names: Hansen, Grace, author.

Title: Military amphibious vehicles / by Grace Hansen.

Description: Minneapolis, Minnesota : Abdo Kids, 2017 | Series: Military aircraft
    & vehicles | Includes bibliographical references and index.

Identifiers: LCCN 2016944106 | ISBN 9781680809329 (lib. bdg.) |
    ISBN 9781680796421 (ebook) | ISBN 9781680797091 (Read-to-me ebook)

Subjects: LCSH: Motor vehicles, Amphibious--Juvenile literature. | Military
    vehicles--Juvenile literature.

Classification: DDC 623.825--dc23

LC record available at http://lccn.loc.gov/2016944106

Table of Contents

Water to Land!

Militaries use amphibious vehicles. These are vehicles that work on both water and land.

AAV

An **AAV** is mobile and armed.

It has tracks to move on land.

But it also has motors to

move in water.

AAVs are usually the first vehicles to land during beach **raids**. They can carry 21 **marines** and three crewmembers. They also carry 10,000 pounds (4,536 kg) of cargo.

LARC-V

An **LARC-V** carries cargo over land and sea. It uses wheels to move on land.

LARC-Vs can reach speeds of 9.5 mph (15 km/h) on water. On land, they can move 30 mph (48 km/h).

13

BTR-80

A **BTR**-80 is an armored personnel carrier. Its main job is to get soldiers to the battlefield. It also gives close fire support.

A **BTR**-80 can carry a commander, driver, gunner, and seven other soldiers. It is quite slow on water, but can move up to 55 mph (68 km/h) on land with its eight wheels.

LCAC

An **LCAC** uses air to move over water and land. It brings personnel to shore. It also brings weapons and cargo.

87

19

LCACs leave ships 50 miles (80 km) offshore. This keeps military ships at a safe distance. LCACs can move 40 mph (64 km/h) with a full load.

20

Landing Craft, Air Cushion (LCAC) Up Close

- Crew: 5

- Capacity: 60 tons (54,431 kg)

- Speed: 40+ knots with **payload**

four-bladed propellers

- Cruise range with payload: 200 miles (322 km)

- Cruise range without payload: 300 miles (483 km)

22

Glossary

AAV – Assault Amphibious Vehicle.

BTR – is short for Bronyetransporter.

LARC-V – Lighter Amphibian Resupply Cargo V.

LCAC – Landing Craft, Air Cushion.

marine – a member of the US Marine Corps who serves both on ships and on land.

payload – the passengers and other cargo for delivery at a destination.

raid – a sudden assault or attack on the enemy.

23

Index

abdokids.com

Use this code to log on to abdokids.com and access crafts, games, videos, and more!

Abdo Kids Code:
MMK9329